The Fig
on the

The pigs are going
on a picnic.
Mother Pig makes them
one hundred
delicious sandwiches.

The goats are going
on a picnic.
Mother Goat makes them
one hundred
roly-poly hamburgers.

The pigs go up the hill.
They go past
the black rock,
past the rabbit holes,
past the tall flowers,

up, **up, up.**

The goats go up the hill.
They go past
the crooked tree,
past the bumpy rocks,
past the little flowers,

up, **up,** **up.**

The pigs and the goats meet at the top of the hill.

"We will fight you,"
say the goats.

"No, we will fight YOU!"
say the pigs.

The pigs and the goats
begin to fight.

It's
OUR hill.

No, it's
OUR hill.

The goats push the pigs.
The pigs push the goats.
The goats bleat.
The pigs squeal.
There is a terrible fight
going on all over
the top of the hill.

The pigs push over
the goats' basket.
One hundred roly-poly
hamburgers go roly-poly
down the hill.

They go past the little flowers,
past the bumpy rocks,
past the crooked tree,

down,
       down,
              down.

"Oh dear!" cry the goats.
"There goes our picnic."

Now the pigs feel sorry
for the goats.
"Have some of our
sandwiches," say the pigs.
"We've got plenty."

The goats have a picnic
after all.
"It's silly to fight,"
say the pigs.
"It doesn't matter
who was first to the top."

"Yes, it's silly to fight,"
say the goats.
"There's plenty of room
for everyone on top
of the hill."

The picnic is over.
The pigs and the goats
go down the hill
to the goats' house.

"Mum, we've brought
our friends home,"
say the goats.
"What's for dinner?"

"Guess what,"
says Mother Goat.
"Our dinner came rolling
down the hill,
along the path,
through the door,
and into the kitchen...

one hundred dusty,
roly-poly hamburgers!"